Your Government

by Ted Silveira

A Pacemaker® Book

GLOBE FEARON
Pearson Learning Group

Photo credits:
Cover: UPI
Page 2: UPI
Page 4: George Bellerose/Stock, Boston
Page 6: Wide World Photos
Page 11: Owen D. B./Black Star
Page 11: Wide World Photos
Page 18: UPI
Page 20: Owen J. T./Black Star
Page 26: Wide World Photos
Page 30: Wide World Photos
Page 32: Wide World Photos
Page 34: UPI
Page 37: Wide World Photos
Page 37: Wide World Photos
Page 42: Wide World Photos
Page 48: UPI
Page 50: Wide World Photos
Page 57: Flip Schulke/Black Star
Page 60: W. B. Finch/Stock, Boston
Page 63: © Louis Dematteis
Page 65: Wide World Photos
Page 69: Tom Sobolik/Black Star
Page 73: Emilio Mercado/Jeroboam, Inc.
Page 74: Ellis Herwig/Stock, Boston

FEARON/JANUS/QUERCUS gratefully acknowledges Nicholas Johnson
for writing portions of this book.

ISBN 0-8224-7679-7

Printed in the United States of America

15 16 17 18 19 20   06 05 04 03 02

Globe
Fearon
Pearson Learning Group

1-800-321-3106
www.pearsonlearning.com

Contents

Introduction

What do you think of when you hear the word *government*? You might think of the president of the United States. Or you might think of your governor or mayor. All three are working in some form of government. In this book, you'll learn about these different forms of government. But for a start, try to think of *government* as a system that shapes the way people live. In some countries, the people work for the system. In the United States, the system works for the people.

The people choose leaders to run the government for them. They choose lawmakers who will make the laws they want. And the people have much to say about the important decisions their government makes. But to make these important decisions, they need to know how the government works.

People who know how the government works can choose good leaders to run it for them. They can make good decisions about what the government should do. And they can make sure that the government really does what the people want it to do. This power belongs to you, your neighbors, and all Americans. It's your government. This book will help you take part in it.

Part 1

YOUR FEDERAL GOVERNMENT

Chapter 1

THE CONSTITUTION

Words to Know

amendments changes and additions to the Constitution

article a part of a written work; there are seven articles in the Constitution of the United States

bill of rights a list of rights promised to the people of a country; the United States Bill of Rights is the first 10 amendments to the Constitution

checks and balances a system of government that gives each branch some control over the power of the other branches

executive branch the part of the government that carries out the laws

federal government the central government of a country

judicial branch the part of the government that rules on what the laws mean

legislative branch the part of the government that makes the laws

representative democracy a kind of government in which groups of people choose people to act and speak for them

representatives people who act and speak for others; members of the House of Representatives

veto the power of the president to stop a law from passing

On Independence Day, July 4, 1788, the people of Philadelphia were ready for a holiday. The city was putting on a parade. Down the stone streets rumbled a horse-drawn wagon. On the wagon was a model ship with a sign that read, "Constitution." People greeted the ship with wild cheers as it passed. The ship meant more to them than anything else in the parade.

What was going on? Why were the people cheering for a model ship named the *Constitution*? In fact, they were really cheering for something that had happened the year before.

In May 1787, a group of people had traveled to Philadelphia from the 13 states that formed the United States of America. Many had come hundreds of miles on horseback to be there. Most had come because they were worried. They had feared that their government was not strong enough to hold the 13 states together. They had come to talk about ways to patch up the government.

For three and a half months, these people had talked and joked and argued. At times, their meetings had turned into a war of words. But when they left the city in September, they had written out plans for a completely new government. The plan itself was called the Constitution of the United States.

When the people of Philadelphia saw the model ship on Independence Day in 1788, they were cheering for the new government of the United States. The people were looking ahead to a better future. They were hoping they finally had a government that would work.

Today, some 200 years later, we no longer hold parades to cheer the Constitution. But the Constitution has as much meaning for us as it did for the people in 1788. It remains the most important piece of writing in American history. It is still the highest law of the land.

A Government of the People

If you were writing rules for a club you belonged to, what would you say? How would you put your ideas in order? How many rules would you list? Would they be general or full of small details?

The writers of the Constitution had to answer some of the same questions. They decided to write the Constitution with seven parts. Each part is called an *article*. The seven articles describe a very general plan, a sort of outline of government. They tell who makes and carries out the laws and how this is done.

The most important idea in the Constitution is in the very first sentence. It says that the power of the government comes from the people. The government can act only in the interests of the people.

In 1863, President Abraham Lincoln described this idea in another way. He called ours a "government of the people, by the people, for the people." He meant that the United States government:

- belongs to the people

- is run according to the wishes of the people

- serves the people

In the United States, then, the people rule. But how?

In some small New England towns, all the people of the town hold meetings to decide how the town government should be

In a democracy everyone has a say in how the government is run, like these citizens of a small village in Vermont.

run. Everyone votes on all the town laws. But even in 1787, this plan would not have worked for the **federal government**. The country was too big to have everyone vote on every law.

Another kind of plan was set up. In this plan, the people choose **representatives** to make laws for them. The representatives speak and act for large groups of people. We call this kind of government a **representative democracy**.

A System of Many Governments

Before the Constitution was written, the states had many powers. Each state could coin its own money. Each one could tax things people brought in from other states. But soon the states started arguing with one another. The federal government could do little to bring peace. It did not have enough power to stop these fights.

The writers of the Constitution tried to solve the problem. In some cases, they took powers away from the states and gave them to the federal government. The Constitution did not give any new powers to the states. Instead, it made the power of the federal government much stronger.

The Constitution writers were concerned mostly about balancing power between the states and the federal government. But they also knew that every city and town needed some power to make its own laws. So they set up a plan for government on three levels. The same plan is used today.

- *Federal government.* The federal government has control over matters that concern the whole country. Only the federal government has the power to coin money or declare war.

- *State government.* Each of the 50 states has a state government. It decides matters that concern people in every part of the state. A state government has the power to make laws that say young people must go to school until they reach a certain age.

- *Local government.* Each of the thousands of counties, cities, and towns has a government. It deals with local matters, such as traffic laws and building laws.

This system of three levels of government is a system of shared power. Most Americans like it that way. It is a way of limiting the power of any one group.

Nine judges sit on the Supreme Court that makes up the judicial branch of the government.

Three Branches of Government

The writers of the Constitution also found a way to limit power *within* the federal government. They split the power of this government among three groups, called branches.

- The **legislative branch** makes the laws. This branch is called the Congress of the United States. The Congress is made up of two parts called houses—the House of Representatives and the Senate.

- The **executive branch** carries out the laws. The president of the United States is in charge of this branch. The vice president helps the president.

- The **judicial branch** decides whether the laws follow the meaning of the Constitution. The United States Supreme Court heads this branch. Nine judges serve on the Court.

The writers of the Constitution believed that it was important for each branch to have separate powers. Why? They thought that each branch would keep the others from getting too powerful. Each branch would check, or put controls on, the actions of the others. And each branch would balance, or have the same amount of power, as the others.

How does this system of **checks and balances** work? Let's suppose the legislative branch, or Congress, wants to pass a new law. But the executive branch, or president, does not agree with it. The president decides to **veto** this law and stop it from passing. The executive branch has "checked" the legislative branch and has stopped it from acting.

But sometimes the legislative branch can still pass the law. When the president vetoes a law, Congress can vote on it again. If enough people in Congress agree with it, the law is passed. In this way, the legislative branch can check the executive branch.

Now let's suppose the legislative and executive branches have passed the law. But the judicial branch, or the Supreme Court, decides that the law goes against the Constitution. The judges can stop the law from being carried out. In this way, the judicial branch checks the legislative and executive branches.

Have you ever been able to guess what will happen in the future? Maybe you have guessed a grade that you got on a test or whether you'd get a summer job. But can you guess what you will be doing 10 years from now? Or 20 years from now?

The writers of the Constitution tried to see far into the future. They knew the country would probably grow in size. They hoped it would grow in other ways too. But they could not guess what the country would be like in 100 years, or 200 years. How could they be sure that the Constitution would still work in the years to come?

They knew the federal government had to change as the country changed. So they came up with a plan for changing the Constitution and adding to it. These changes to the Constitution are called **amendments**.

Americans lost little time putting this plan into action. By 1791, they had added 10 amendments to the Constitution. Most of these first 10 amendments promise the American people certain rights. Today we call them the **Bill of Rights**.

Here are a few of the rights and freedoms they give us:

- *Freedom of religion.* The government cannot tell you what church to go to. You can practice the religion of your choice.

- *Freedom of speech.* The government cannot keep you from saying what you like as long as you don't harm others by saying things you know are not true.

- *Freedom of the press.* The government cannot tell writers of newspapers, magazines, or books what to put in their work.

- *Freedom of assembly.* The government cannot keep you from holding peaceful meetings to talk about changes in government.

Those are just a few of the promises made in the Bill of Rights. Since 1791, Americans have added 16 more amendments to the Constitution. The amendments are proof that the Constitution can change as the country changes. For that reason, the Constitution is as important today as it was 200 years ago.

A Lasting Government

Do You Know?

You can see the Constitution and the Bill of Rights in the National Archives in Washington, D.C. They are sealed in glass and metal cases.

Exercise 1

Decide which branch of government is best described by each sentence below. Then in the blank write *E* for the executive branch, *L* for the legislative branch, or *J* for the judicial branch.

_____ 1. It decides whether the laws follow the Constitution.

_____ 2. It is headed by the president of the United States.

_____ 3. It is headed by the United States Supreme Court.

_____ 4. It can pass a law even after the president has vetoed it.

_____ 5. It has the power to veto a law Congress wants to pass.

_____ 6. It is called the Congress of the United States.

_____ 7. It has nine judges.

_____ 8. It carries out the laws.

_____ 9. It is made up of a Senate and a House of Representatives.

_____ 10. It makes the laws.

_____ 11. It can check the actions of Congress.

_____ 12. It includes the vice president.

Chapter 2

MAKING THE GOVERNMENT WORK

Words to Know

budget   a plan for spending money

cabinet   a group made up of the heads of 13 different executive departments in the federal government

ceremonial   done in a formal way for a special or important occasion

citizen   a member of a country

councils   groups of people called together to give the president their ideas

diplomats   government workers trained to deal with governments of other countries

elected   chosen by the people; voted into office

independent agencies   government groups that study special problems and make rules about them

popular   well known and well liked by many people

term   the length of time a person holds government office; the president's term is four years

His name is printed almost every day in the newspapers. His face is seen almost every night on the television news. The president of the United States is known to millions of people around the world. He makes news in many different ways.

Maybe he has just thrown out the first baseball of the season. Or gone to Texas to ask people to vote for a woman running for office there. Or met with leaders from other countries to talk about world trade. Or asked for a new law to protect wildlife.

Some people say the job of president is the toughest job in the world. When things go smoothly, the president is a **popular** leader. But when they don't, he often must take much of the blame. Because of the many problems a president faces, understanding why anyone would want the job is hard sometimes. Yet every four years, many people try for the job.

Laws about Being President

The Constitution says very little about who can be president. It tells us that the president must:

- be a "natural born **citizen**" (either born in the United States or born outside the United States to parents who were already citizens of the United States)

- be 35 years of age or older

- have lived in the United States for at least 14 years

Other laws limit the power of the president. One of them sets the number of years a person can be president. A presidential **term** lasts four years. Once a person is **elected** president, that person can hold that office again for only one more term. This means that no president can hold that office longer than two terms, or eight years.

The Jobs of the President

The president, of course, is head of the executive branch of the federal government. But his responsibilities do not stop there. The president has six kinds of jobs to do.

Do You Know?

In 1960, John F. Kennedy became the youngest elected president. He was 43 years old. In 1980, Ronald Reagan became the oldest elected president. He was 69 years old.

Chief Executive The Constitution gives the president power to carry out the laws. As chief executive, the president chooses people to help him run the government. He makes key decisions about what the government will and will not do. He also keeps track of the ways the government spends money. He does this by drawing up a spending plan called a **budget**.

Chief of State In some countries a king or queen handles certain jobs. He or she greets important visitors, gives speeches on important holidays, and tries to be a good example for the country as a whole. Greeting a visitor and giving a speech are **ceremonial** jobs. In the United States, there is no king or queen to handle them. As chief of state, the president carries out many ceremonial jobs himself.

Chief Diplomat **Diplomats** are government workers trained to deal with other countries. As the chief diplomat, the president is in charge of keeping peace. He decides what agreements the United States will reach with other governments. And he tries to keep the United States on a friendly course with countries around the world.

As chief of state, then-President Jimmy Carter greets Pope John Paul II in the Oval Office at the White House.

As chief diplomat, President Ronald Reagan inspects a Guard of Honour on Reagan's official visit to Windsor Castle with Prince Philip.

Commander-in-Chief The president is not a member of the armed forces—neither the army, navy, air force, marines, nor any other branch. Yet he has charge of all those forces. He gives orders to the leaders of the armed forces. He can send troops to any part of the United States in case of trouble. He can send troops to different parts of the world.

Chief Lawmaker Congress, of course, makes the laws. But the president can say what laws he would like to have passed. Today most presidents send ideas for new laws to the legislative branch. In some cases, they do this by delivering special messages to Congress.

Party Chief Some presidents have been members of the Republican party. Others have belonged to the Democratic party. But no matter which party the president belongs to, he is clearly the leader of his party. To be chosen president, he must have the support of other party members. To get their support, he must work for the party and help party members who are running for other offices. To be successful in getting laws passed, he must work closely with members of his party in Congress.

The president lives in the most famous home in the land—the White House in Washington, D.C. The White House is not only his home. It is also his office. The most trusted people on his team work there.

The President's Team

Lights often burn late in the White House. Sometimes the president must struggle with problems far into the night. He is boss of so many people that he cannot even count them. The number of offices in his control is so large that no city phone book could list them all. How can he handle such a huge job?

The answer is that the president doesn't handle the job alone. He counts on other leaders in the federal government to help him get the job done. In some cases, they give him the facts he needs to make a decision. In other cases, they help shape his thinking.

The chart on the next page shows four groups or offices that make up the president's team. Depending on the decision to be made, the president might meet with:

- the vice president
- **cabinet** members
- the heads of **independent agencies**
- members of special **councils**

The Vice President

In some ways, the vice president should be the person closest to the president. The vice president has been elected to office along with the president. In most cases, he also has been picked by the president himself to run for the office.

But even so, the vice president is not usually the closest member of the president's team. He has far less power than the president does. The vice president's main job is to serve as the leader of the United States Senate. But the real importance of the vice president is his responsibility to take over the president's job when the president can no longer do it. If the president becomes very ill or dies in office, the vice president must take his place.

The President's Cabinet

Usually once a week, the president holds a cabinet meeting in the White House. The size of the group changes from week to week. But 13 people are almost always there. They are the heads of the 13 different cabinet departments. The names of these departments are on the chart on page 13.

All department heads are known as secretaries, except the head of the Department of Justice, who is called the attorney general. These people are a special group chosen by the president, so he is their boss. They often give him the facts he needs to make decisions.

Suppose the president learns that all railroad workers are planning to stop working until they get new safety rules. The secretary of transportation might ask the president to step in and force the workers to stay on the job. Otherwise many businesses will get hurt if all the trains are at a standstill for days, or even weeks. But the secretary of labor might ask the president to think about the workers' needs. The new safety rules will protect the workers as well as the passengers. The attorney general then tells the president what he can and cannot do under the law. The president listens carefully to each of these people. Then he decides how to act.

But the cabinet members do not really spend much of their time talking with the president. Most of the time, they are directing the important work of their departments. The name of each department and what it does are shown on the chart below.

Chart of the Executive Branch

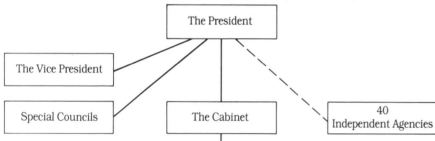

The Cabinet Departments

State
- Deals with governments of other countries

Justice
- Presents the government's case in all federal trials

Housing & Urban Development
- Makes rules about run-down neighborhoods
- Helps build low-rent housing

Commerce
- Makes rules about goods that are sold or moved across state lines

Treasury
- Collects taxes
- Coins and prints money
- Controls banks

Interior
- Manages public lands
- Runs national parks

Labor
- Helps people who are out of work
- Helps settle problems between workers and bosses

Education
- Helps states pay for many different kinds of school programs

Energy
- Tries to make sure there is enough gas, coal, oil and other kinds of energy

Defense
- Protects the country from attack
- Runs the armed forces

Agriculture
- Helps farmers and farming in many different ways

Health & Human Services
- Sends monthly checks to people who are past working age
- Checks food and drugs for safety

Transportation
- Builds and keeps up federal highways
- Checks safety of airplanes

Independent Agencies

The federal government has more than 40 independent agencies that study special problems and make rules about them. One of these agencies is the Food and Drug Administration. It sets rules about what may go into the food and medicines that we use.

Unlike cabinet secretaries and their departments, agencies do not take orders from the president. His only power over these agencies is that he chooses the people who run them. For this reason, the agencies are thought of as independent. Each agency is free to set down rules about anything that is within its responsibilities. But these rules must be within the limits of the law.

Special Councils

The president gets help from a number of special councils. These councils come up with plans for the president to think about. Among the special councils is the National Security Council. It makes plans for the defense of the country. The National Security Council has only six members.

Another special council is the White House Office. It is a very large council made up of the people closest to the president. Some of them write speeches. Others answer letters. Still others set up the president's trips.

The President and the People

Do You Know?

The White House receives about 20,000 letters every day.

The president listens to the White House Office. He hears what his cabinet members have to say. He reads what newspapers write about him. He learns what the television news reports about him.

All of this is important. Yet none of it is quite as important as knowing what most Americans think. To be successful, a president must be popular. And to be popular, he needs to understand what the people think.

How does he find out what people are thinking? He reads some of the letters that are sent to the White House. He also reads different studies that report how many people are for and against one matter or another. Above all, he travels all across the country talking to voters. He know that his biggest job as president is to follow the will of the people.

Exercise 2

Read each problem described below. Decide which cabinet department would handle the problem. Then write the name of the department in the blank. Use the chart on page 13 for help.

_____ 1. More money is needed to pay for a school program.

_____ 2. Many farmers' crops have been ruined by a large flood.

_____ 3. More federal highways are needed.

_____ 4. A leader of another country is angry about an action taken by the United States.

_____ 5. Banks say that they need more 100-dollar bills.

_____ 6. Checks sent to people who are past working age are missing.

_____ 7. There isn't enough money to keep up the country's national parks.

_____ 8. The air force needs new and better planes.

_____ 9. The country is running out of gas, coal, and oil.

_____ 10. There is not enough low-rent housing for the people who need it.

Chapter 3

THE PEOPLE WHO MAKE THE LAWS

Words to Know

bills   ideas for new laws that are written up and voted on

committees   groups of people in Congress who meet to learn about certain problems and find ways to solve them

majority   more than half

president pro tempore   the leader of the Senate when the vice president is away

senators   members of the Senate

session   the day-to-day meetings of Congress that are held during most of the year

standing committee   committees in the House and the Senate that keep studying the same kinds of problems even though the committee members may change from one election to the next

Have you ever questioned why a letter took so long to be delivered? Or wondered why so much money was taken out of your paycheck to pay taxes? If so, you may have said, "There ought to be a law!"

Only one branch of the federal government can decide if "there ought to be a law." It is the Congress of the United States. Congress is often called the "people's branch" of government. Unlike most federal office-holders, all members of Congress are chosen by the people. That is why they are said to be the federal leaders closest to us all.

Who are these members of Congress? They come from every part of the country and from many different walks of life. They are men and women of many different races and religions. About half are lawyers. But some have been truck drivers and baseball players. Those who enter Congress do not reach it by any single path. But they all enter Congress to do one important job—to make our country's laws.

Each year in early January, Congress begins a new **session**. Sessions are made up of day-to-day meetings that are held during most of the year. These meetings take place in a huge, white building in Washington, D.C. This building, the Capitol, sits on top of a hill in the center of the city. It has hundreds of offices and rooms for both houses of Congress to meet.

On most days, the Capitol is one of the busiest places in America. And it isn't hard to understand why. During each session, the Senate and the House of Representatives review more than 10,000 ideas for new laws. These ideas are known as **bills**. Out of these 10,000 bills, usually only a few hundred become laws. But every bill that becomes a law must be voted on by members of each house.

Congress in Session

The House of Representatives is the larger house of Congress. It has 435 voting members called representatives. Each one represents a certain number of people in a state. The more people a state has, the more representatives it sends to Congress. Rhode Island, which has about one million people, sends two representatives. California, which has more than 24 million people, sends 45 representatives.

To serve in the House, a person must:

- be at least 25 years old
- have been a citizen of the United States for at least seven years
- live in the state from which he or she is chosen

The House of Representatives is also called the lower house of Congress. Representatives serve shorter terms and represent fewer people than members of the Senate. Each representative is elected by the people in a certain area of a state. And a representative serves for two years. Because their representatives are up for election every other year, the voters often have the chance to judge the work their representatives are doing. So representatives must follow the wishes of the voters if they want to stay in office for a long time.

Speaker of the House When representatives meet on opening day, they first must choose a leader. Their leader is the Speaker of the House. The Speaker belongs to the party with the

The House of Representatives

most members in the House and is voted in by a **majority** of the House members. Speakers of the House often serve for several terms.

The Speaker has a great deal of power. Much of it comes from being head of the majority party. Among other things, the Speaker decides or helps to decide:

- who will study each bill that comes to the House

- who may speak to the House and when

- how House rules are to be judged and put to use

- when a vote of the whole House should be taken

Another part of the Speaker's power is described in the Constitution. If the president and vice president cannot continue in their jobs, the Speaker becomes president of the United States. The Speaker is said to be the second most important person in the federal government.

The dome of the Capital, one of the largest in the world, can be seen for miles around Washington, D.C.

The Senate

The Senate is much smaller than the House of Representatives. The Senate has only 100 members—two from each of the 50 states. Members of the Senate are called **senators**. To serve in the Senate, a person must:

- be at least 30 years old
- have been a citizen of the United States for nine years or more
- live in the state from which he or she has been chosen

The Senate is also called the upper house of Congress. A senator represents more people than a representative because a senator is elected by all the people in a state. And members of the Senate serve for six years—three times longer than representatives. Because they don't have to try to get elected as often, senators do not have to follow the voters' wishes as closely as representatives do. Senators are freer to make decisions based on what they think will be good for the country in the years ahead.

President of the Senate The senators' leader is the president of the Senate. The Constitution gives this job to the vice president of the United States. The vice president helps to decide:

- who may or may not speak to the Senate
- when a vote should be taken on a certain bill

But the vice president does not have as much power as the Speaker of the House. He is not a member of the Senate. He cannot speak for or against a bill. He can vote *only* to break a tie. And he does not have to vote even then.

Today, a vice president has many other jobs besides being president of the Senate. So when he is away on other business, his place in the Senate usually is taken by the **president pro tempore**. (*Pro tempore* means "for the time being.") This leader is an important member of the Senate and usually has been elected to the Senate several times.

Committees of Congress

Leaders of the House and the Senate help Congress get through a great load of work. Yet they are not the only keys to getting things done. Much of the day-to-day work in both houses is done by **committees**. These groups study different kinds of problems facing the country. Every member of Congress serves

The vice president serves as president of the Senate. Here Vice President George Bush presides over a meeting of Congressional leaders.

Do You Know?

The third person in line for the president's job is the president pro tempore. In 1849, President pro tempore David Rice Atchison was president for one day. President Polk and his vice president left office on Saturday, but newly-elected President Taylor and his vice president didn't take office until Monday.

on at least one committee. The committees meet to learn about a problem, solve it, or take some other action.

The most important committees in Congress are **standing committees**. The House has about 20 standing committees. The Senate usually doesn't have quite as many. The standing committee members may change from one election to the next, but the kinds of problems each committee studies stay the same.

Each standing committee has a special interest. One Senate committee may study bills having to do only with the army and navy. One House committee may study bills about the post office. Committees gather as many facts as possible before deciding on a bill. They listen to people speaking for and against it. Then committee members discuss the bill among themselves.

At last they take a vote on the bill. If most of them vote for it, the bill then goes to the House or Senate for a final vote. But if most committee members do not like a bill, the bill will never leave the committee. The full House or Senate will not hear about the bill for that term.

In this way, the representatives and senators on committees have a lot of power. They decide which bills will have a chance to become laws and which ones won't. And this power can make a big difference in how the country is run.

Exercise 3

Decide whether the people described below could be senators or representatives, or whether they could be either. Then in each blank write *S* for Senator, *R* for Representative, or *E* for either.

_____ 1. Barbara Cox was 29 years old when she entered Congress.

_____ 2. Mark Kramer has ended the third year of his first term in Congress.

_____ 3. David Kowalski, Eliott Johnson, Mildred Frank, and Stewart Wong all live in the same state and serve in the same house of Congress.

_____ 4. Patrick Altman has just finished his first year as Speaker.

_____ 5. Maria Fernandez is the head of a standing committee.

_____ 6. When Andrew Marino was first elected, he had been a citizen for eight years.

_____ 7. Matt Davidson is president pro tempore.

_____ 8. After 12 years in Congress, Shirley Jones has finished her second term.

_____ 9. California has only two representatives in this house.

_____ 10. Marilyn Richards serves on two different committees.

Chapter 4

MAKING OUR COUNTRY'S LAWS

Words to Know

debate   to talk or agree about the good and bad points of something

represent   to act or speak for another person or a group of people

taxes   money paid by people or businesses to the government; this money pays for the work that the government does

Your members in Congress have been elected to **represent** you and the people from your state. So their job is to make sure that government meets your special needs. This job means talking to companies about doing business with our state. It means meeting important visitors from other countries. And it means working with special groups who need help from the federal government.

But the most important job of members of Congress is to make new laws. Your representatives and senators will try to pass laws that will be good for you and your state. And they will vote against laws that will hurt your state. But if all the members of Congress are trying to make laws that are good for their own states, how can they make laws that are good for the whole country? For that matter, how can the 535 members of Congress agree on any law at all?

Every law must be agreed on by a majority—more than half— of the members of Congress. The majority would not agree to a law that might be good for your state but bad for the other 49 states. So if most of them agree on a law, it probably is good for most people in the country. But getting so many members to agree on a law isn't easy. It takes a lot of talking, a lot of give-and-take, and almost always some changes.

Every law begins as a bill in the House of Representatives or in the Senate. No matter which house the bill starts in, it must go through six important steps to become a law. These steps are shown on the chart on the next page.

These steps are shown on the chart on the next page.

1. The Bill Suppose John Atkins, a representative from Massachusetts, has an idea for a new law. He sees that many companies in his state aren't making enough money to keep people working. So many of the people Atkins represents are losing their jobs. He wants to cut the companies' federal **taxes** so that they can save money. But he only wants tax cuts for companies that will use their savings to hire more workers.

Atkins writes his idea down in a bill. He carefully explains which taxes should be cut and what the companies must do to get the tax cut. Then he sends the bill to his own house, the House of Representatives.

2. The Committee When a bill is given to a house of Congress, it goes first to a committee—a small group made up of members from both parties.

Atkins's bill goes to the committee that deals with taxes, the House Ways and Means Committee. The committee members study the bill carefully and listen to Atkins explain how the bill would work. They also listen to people who don't think companies should get special tax breaks. And the committee members ask questions: Will this bill do any good? Will it do any harm? Is there a better way to do the same thing?

Finally the committee votes: should they pass the bill or kill it? The members don't all agree, but a majority votes for it. Now the bill goes before all the members of the House.

3. The Debate Now all members of the House of Representatives have a chance to **debate** the bill. They can speak for it or against it, for up to one hour each. And they can try to change the bill by adding amendments to it.

Atkins speaks first and asks the House to pass his bill. A representative from Kansas answers. He says that the bill will not help Kansas, which is mostly a farming state with few big businesses. And besides, if businesses get tax breaks, farmers should too.

A representative from New York speaks. She says that if taxes are cut, the federal government will have less money. Then federal help for poor people may be cut.

How a Law Is Made

How a Bill Becomes a Law

A bill can start in either the House of Representatives or the Senate. The bill shown here starts in the House of Representatives.

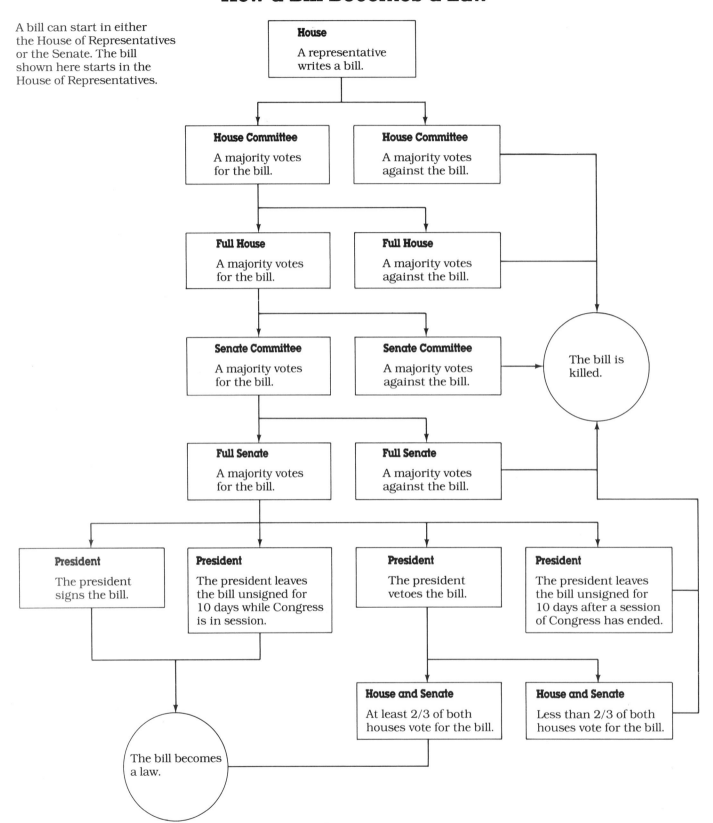

House
A representative writes a bill.

House Committee
A majority votes for the bill.

House Committee
A majority votes against the bill.

Full House
A majority votes for the bill.

Full House
A majority votes against the bill.

Senate Committee
A majority votes for the bill.

Senate Committee
A majority votes against the bill.

The bill is killed.

Full Senate
A majority votes for the bill.

Full Senate
A majority votes against the bill.

President
The president signs the bill.

President
The president leaves the bill unsigned for 10 days while Congress is in session.

President
The president vetoes the bill.

President
The president leaves the bill unsigned for 10 days after a session of Congress has ended.

House and Senate
At least 2/3 of both houses vote for the bill.

House and Senate
Less than 2/3 of both houses vote for the bill.

The bill becomes a law.

A representative from Texas speaks for the bill. She says that lower taxes will help companies grow. And if they grow, they will have more jobs for people. And more work will start up for other businesses, such as trucking and building companies.

The talking goes on for hours. Finally the House votes—235 are for the bill, 200 are against it. The House has passed the bill. It is almost halfway to becoming a law.

4. The Other House Atkins's bill has passed the House, so it goes to the Senate. It goes first to the Finance Committee, which studies tax bills for the Senate. This committee passes the bill and sends it to the full Senate, where debate begins again.

As before, many members from the states without many companies speak against the bill. They're afraid that a lower tax on companies will mean a higher tax on other groups. But senators from big-business states again speak up for the bill.

Finally a senator from Iowa adds an amendment to the bill. The amendment lowers the size of the tax cut. Now more senators agree to vote for the bill. It is passed by the full Senate, but just barely.

5. The Final Bill Representative Atkins's tax has passed both houses of Congress. But an amendment was added to it in the Senate, so the two houses didn't vote on the same bill. The Senate bill is different from the House bill. What happens now?

A special committee with members from both houses must meet to work out the differences between the two bills. These meetings can lead to some very angry words. So the committee meets in secret and keeps no record of what is said. After much work, the committee makes some changes to the amendment so that both the House and Senate members will agree. Now the final bill must be voted on by the full House and by the full Senate. But this time, no more amendments can be added.

Because of the changes, some members of both houses who once voted against the bill now vote for it. The bill passes with a larger majority. It is almost a law.

6. The President Atkins's bill now goes to the president of the United States. The president has the power to look over every bill that Congress passes and to do one of four things:

- The president can sign the bill, making it a law.

- The president can veto the bill. In this case, the bill goes back to Congress. If two-thirds of each house votes for the bill again, it becomes a law even though the president's vetoed it.

Do You Know?

Unlike representatives, senators are allowed to speak more than one hour on a bill. In 1953, Senator Wayne Morse of Oregon made the longest ever nonstop speech in the Senate. He spoke against a bill for 22 hours and 26 minutes without sitting down.

• The president can leave the bill unsigned for 10 days while Congress is in session. In this case, the bill becomes a law even though the president didn't sign it.

• The president can leave the bill unsigned for 10 days after a session of Congress has ended. In this case, the bill dies.

Because Atkins's bill has more backers with its new amendment, the president thinks it's probably a good bill for most of the country. He decides to sign it. Representative Atkins's bill is now a law.

Law Making

It takes months of hard work to make a bill into a law. And many bills that would have helped some people have been killed because not enough people backed them. When each member of Congress is protecting the special interests of the people he or she represents, getting a majority vote for *any* bill is hard.

There's a good reason why making a new law is hard. If it was easy, then every group of people with a special interest might have laws to help it out. But many of these laws might not be good for the country as a whole. So the Constitution says that a majority of people representing all parts of the country must agree to make a new law. In that way, any new law is more likely to be good for the whole country, not just one part.

Surrounded by leaders in the House and Senate, President Lyndon Johnson signed the Civil Rights Bill into law in 1964.

Exercise 4

Follow the steps of a bill that begins in the Senate. In each group below, number the steps from 1 to 4 in the order they happen. Write 1 in the blank beside the first step, 2 beside the second, and so on.

Group 1

_____ (a) The Senate committee passes the bill.

_____ (b) An amendment is added to the bill during the full Senate debate.

_____ (c) A senator writes down an idea for a new law in a bill.

_____ (d) The bill is studied by a Senate committee.

Group 2

_____ (a) The full House debates the bill for hours.

_____ (b) The Senate bill goes to a committee in the House of Representatives.

_____ (c) The House committee votes on the bill and passes it.

_____ (d) The full Senate votes on the bill and passes it.

Group 3

_____ (a) A special committee works out the differences between the House bill and the Senate bill.

_____ (b) A majority of the full House votes for the bill.

_____ (c) Both houses pass the bill as changed by the special committee.

_____ (d) The full House adds another amendment to the bill.

Group 4

_____ (a) The bill becomes a law.

_____ (b) The president vetoes the bill.

_____ (c) The bill that passed both houses of Congress goes to the president.

_____ (d) The bill goes back to both houses of Congress and is passed by a two-thirds majority of each house.

Chapter 5

REVIEWING THE LAWS

Words to Know

appeal   to ask a higher court to review a lower court's decision

guilty   judged as having done something wrong or against the law

jury   in a court of law, a group of people chosen to decide whether someone has broken the law

justices   the judges who are members of the United States Supreme Court

legal   not against the law

public   having to do with the people as a whole; run by the government; public schools are open to everyone

sentence   punishment set by a court of law for a crime, such as a jail term or a fine

Voices fall silent in the crowded courtroom. An officer of the court tells everyone to stand up. Someone pulls back a pair of red curtains. Nine people wearing long, black robes enter the room, ready for another working day. All of them have been chosen by the president. And they have their jobs for life, if they want. In our history, all have been lawyers, and most have been judges.

These nine people are the **justices** of the United States Supreme Court, led by the chief justice. Together the nine justices head the federal court system. They have the final decision on what the Constitution means and whether a law follows the Constitution. And the cases they decide are often very important ones—cases that touch the lives of many people.

There are three main kinds of federal courts. The district courts are the lowest courts in the federal system. The courts of appeals are the next highest. And the United States Supreme Court is the highest court of all.

These federal courts handle three main kinds of cases:

- *Cases dealing with the Constitution.* Federal courts handle questions about the meaning of the Constitution. And they also decide cases about a person or a group that has done something that may be against the Constitution.

- *Cases dealing with federal laws.* Federal courts decide all cases that have to do with federal laws, such as cases about people who don't pay their federal taxes.

- *Cases dealing with more than one state.* If a case deals with people or laws from more than one state, the federal court takes over. A case about a car crash in Texas between two Texans would have to go to a state court. But if one person was from Texas and the other was from Montana, the case could go to federal court.

The Federal Court System

The lowest federal courts are the district courts. There are now 93 of these courts spread across the United States—at least one in each state and up to four in some states. Most federal cases begin in these courts.

District court trials have just one judge. Before and during a trial, the judge looks over the facts and decides which facts can be presented in court. The judge also makes sure that everyone follows the rules. In some cases, the district court judge also decides who is right and who is wrong. But in other cases, the decision must be made by a **jury** of 12 local people chosen for a trial. Either way, the judge decides what the **sentence** will be if someone is found **guilty**.

United States District Courts

Do You Know?

William O. Douglas served the longest term of any Supreme Court justice—36 years (from 1939 to 1975).

The Federal Court System

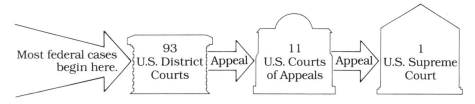

Most federal cases begin here. → 93 U.S. District Courts → Appeal → 11 U.S. Courts of Appeals → Appeal → 1 U.S. Supreme Court

John J. Sirica was the chief judge of one of the 83 U.S. District Courts in Washington, D.C., during the Watergate trial,

United States Courts of Appeals

Sometimes people think they didn't get a fair trial in district court. They think the judge was unfair or the trial didn't follow the rules. What can they do?

These people have a right to **appeal** the district court decision to a higher court. In the federal court system, the next higher court is a United States court of appeals. There are only 11 of these courts spread across the United States because most cases are not appealed.

A judge in the court of appeals first decides if there is a good reason for the appeal. If so, the judge looks over the case and listens to lawyers for each side. He or she checks to see that the lawyers, the first judge, and the jury (if there was one) all followed the law in the right way. If so, the judge will let the district court decision stand. But if the judge thinks a mistake was made, he or she can change the decision or order a new trial.

Suppose the people who appealed their case to the court of appeals are still not happy with the decision. They still feel that the decision is unfair. There is one more court they can go to—the United States Supreme Court. This court is the highest in the land, and its decision can't be changed by any other court.

There is only one Supreme Court. Nine justices work together on the cases. Like the court of appeals, the Supreme Court takes cases only if it believes there is a good reason for the appeal. Even so, the Court handles hundreds of cases each year. And like the court of appeals, the Supreme Court makes sure that the lower courts followed the law and the Constitution.

To make their decision on a case, the justices listen to lawyers from both sides. They look over all the important facts. And they read about earlier cases that were like the present one to find out what other judges have done before. At last, the justices meet alone in a room to decide the case. They each give their thoughts on the case. They question each other closely. Finally they vote. And the decision of the majority is final, even if the vote is 5 to 4.

After the vote, often at least one justice writes a paper explaining the majority decision. But justices who voted against the decision also may write papers to explain their stands. The justices write these paper to help lawyers, judges, and other people understand the reasons for the decision. And these papers are very important because the Supreme Court has the last word on what the law and the Constitution mean.

United States Supreme Court

Since it began, the Supreme Court has decided thousands and thousands of cases. Many cases have shaped our laws and the way we understand our Constitution. But times change, and so do ideas. Sometimes the Court changes its mind about an earlier decision. This happened with a case about the rights of blacks.

The First Decision One day in 1892, a black American named Homer Plessy got on a train in New Orleans, Louisiana. In his day, some state laws set aside different railroad cars for blacks and for whites. So when Plessy took a seat in a car marked "For Whites Only," he was arrested. But Homer Plessy believed that such laws went against the Constitution.

Our Changing Laws

Do You Know?

In 1981, Sandra Day O'Connor became the first woman to serve on the Supreme Court.

When Plessy's case was decided in the Louisiana state courts, he lost. But Plessy appealed to the United States Supreme Court. The Court took the case because it brought up an important question about the Constitution. Did the Louisiana state law take away the rights promised to Homer Plessy in the Constitution?

The Supreme Court ruled that the Louisiana state law was not against the Constitution as long as each railroad car was just as good as the others. The railroad cars for blacks and whites were the same, so Plessy lost his case. And other states used the ruling to keep blacks and whites apart—with separate hotels, separate restaurants, and separate **public** schools.

The Second Decision In the 1950s, some black parents in Topeka, Kansas, tested these state laws again. They believed that the schools for their children were not as good as the schools for white children. Like Homer Plessy, these parents lost their case in the state courts. And like Plessy, they appealed to the United States Supreme Court. Once again, the Court took the case.

But now it was 1954, and both the justices and the people of the country had changed their ideas about what was right. The nine justices ruled that the very idea of public schools for blacks and for whites went against the Constitution. The Court's decision meant that separate schools were not **legal** anywhere in the United States. And the decision showed that the Supreme Court can change as the times change.

Thurgood Marshall (center) was the winning lawyer in the important case against separate schools for blacks. He later became the first black justice on the Supreme Court.

Exercise 5

Decide which court is best described by each sentence below. Then in the blank write *S* for the United States Supreme Court, *A* for a United States court of appeals, *D* for a United States district court, and *X* if the court described is not a federal court.

_____ 1. It is made up of nine justices who are chosen by the president and can serve for life.

_____ 2. It is one of 93 such courts in the United States.

_____ 3. It handles mostly cases dealing with state laws and state constitutions.

_____ 4. It is the lowest court in the federal court system.

_____ 5. In 1954, it struck down state laws that made separate schools for whites and blacks.

_____ 6. It is the first court to which a federal case can be appealed.

_____ 7. It is a court that handles only traffic cases.

_____ 8. It is one of 11 such courts in the United States.

_____ 9. It is headed by the chief justice of the United States.

_____ 10. It is the court in which most federal cases start.

_____ 11. It is the court in which a case between people from the same state probably will start.

_____ 12. It is the last court to which a case can be appealed.

YOUR STATE GOVERNMENT

Chapter 6

THE POWERS OF THE STATES

Words to Know

federal aid   money that the federal government gives to the states to try to solve certain problems

national   having to do with the whole country

pollution   harmful wastes that make the air or water dirty and unhealthy

The United States is one of the biggest countries in the world. It stretches from Maine to California almost 3,000 miles. Then it makes a giant leap across the Pacific Ocean to Hawaii—almost 6,000 miles from Maine. And the distance from the tip of Texas to the northern part of Alaska is almost 7,000 miles. It is no wonder that among the 50 states, there are no two alike.

There are mountain states, plains states, desert states, and coastal states. There are states with very few people and others that are crowded. In some states, many of the people are farmers. In others, most are miners, ranchers, or factory workers. Michigan is known for making cars, Florida for growing oranges, and Maine for its fishing. Every state has something special about it, something that makes it different from any other state.

It is easy to see why the federal government alone cannot handle the special needs of each and every state. The country is too big and the states too different for only one government to do the job. That's why every state has its own state government.

Each state government makes its own state laws and takes care of its own needs. Connecticut may have special laws about air-conditioning in some public buildings, such as hospitals. Minnesota may have special laws about hunting and fishing. Ohio may want more land for state parks, while California may want more land for housing or farming.

A state government takes care of needs like these—needs that may be important only to the people of that state. By letting each state solve its own problems, the federal government is free to take care of things that are important to all people of all states.

Limiting the States' Powers

Most people think of themselves first as Americans and then as members of their states, such as Texans, Californians, or Georgians. Why is that? Part of the reason is that the federal government has much more power than the state governments.

Before the Constitution was written, the first 13 states had many powers that the federal government has today. The states could coin their own money, tax goods that came from other states, and raise their own armies. But the states began to fight among themselves because each state wanted to do things its own way. Without a strong federal government to settle these differences, the same thing would happen today, except that there would be *50* states arguing with each other.

The Constitution ended all this fighting by taking power away from the states. Today a state's power is limited to handling only those matters inside the state, such as schools and police work. Anything that concerns trade, travel, and other business between states is handled by the federal government. That way, the federal government can make sure that all parts of the country work together. This system of balanced power has helped make the country one of the strongest in the world.

State Constitutions

To do its job, a state government needs a set of written laws. So every state has a state constitution—the highest law in the state.

State constitutions are a lot like the United States Constitution. They limit what the state government can do and give final power to the people. Each has a bill of rights that lists the rights of the people. All state constitutions set up state governments that have three branches—executive, legislative, and judicial. And all of them use checks and balances to keep any one branch from having too much power. And like the United States Constitution, the state constitutions can be changed by adding amendments.

The States' Powers

A state constitution describes the powers that the state has inside its own state lines. Each state can pass laws, make sure people follow them, and set up courts to deal with those who don't. A state can raise money by borrowing it or by taxing

It's "midnight at noon" in downtown Pittsburgh, PA, before there were any antipollution laws.

After smog control legislation had been passed by the city government, Pittsburgh soon looked like this.

people and businesses in the state. It can control how people do business in the state. And each state has a strong general power to protect the health, safety, and well-being of its people.

Health A state guards people's health by making rules for restaurants, public swimming pools, and other such places where people could get sick if the places aren't clean. A state can also make rules about air and water **pollution**. And it can set the drinking age and pass laws against sale of illegal drugs.

Safety To guard people's safety, a state can set highway speed limits and safety rules for workers. It can make rules for building safe houses. It can make laws about owning and carrying guns. And it can take steps to fight crime.

Well-being To protect the public's well-being, a state sometimes may have to limit people's freedom. A state can set ages for learning to drive and for getting married. It can say who must go to school and what must be taught. A state can give tests that lawyers, doctors, and other people must pass before they can work. And it can set business hours for bars and make laws about gambling.

Do You Know?

When Texas became a state in 1845, the federal government made a special deal. The deal says Texas can divide itself into as many as four states if it wants to. But this probably will never happen.

Usually a state can make any law it decides the state needs. But the law can't go against the United States Constitution. If it does, the federal government can force the state to drop the law. This happened in 1962 in New York, Pennsylvania, and Maryland. These states had laws that made every public school start the day with a prayer. But the United States Supreme Court ruled that these laws went against the Constitution. The Court said these laws were not in keeping with the right to freedom of religion granted to us in the Bill of Rights. So the states had to give up these laws.

Working with the Federal Government

Do You Know?

In 1981, the federal government sent almost $100 billion in aid to the states.

Most of the time, state and federal governments work separately, each handling its own job. But there are times when they work together to solve either a state or **national** problem.

One problem the country is facing is air pollution. Almost every state has to deal with air made dirty by factories and cars. But suppose only one state tried to do something about it. One state alone could not do much good if neighboring states did nothing to clean up their air. So to solve such a problem, many states have to work together. And that's when the federal government can help.

The federal government can help the state governments by giving them **federal aid**—money for solving a problem like air pollution. First, the federal government sets rules about how clean air has to be. Then it gives each state money—maybe millions of dollars—to help clean up the air. And it lets the states decide just how to spend this money.

Pennsylvania may want to use its money to clean up the air pollution from factories. California might decide to spend its money controlling the pollution from cars. And New York may want to spend its money on new trains so that people won't have to drive their cars as much.

If the federal government forced every state to handle the problem the same way, some states would always lose out. A federal plan to buy more trains could help a crowded area, such as New York City. But it wouldn't help much in areas that have few people. So the federal government lets the states decide how to spend the money. Each state can work to solve its local air pollution problem. And all the states working together can help the federal government solve the country's problem.

Exercise 6

Decide whether a state has the power to do each thing described below. If it does, circle YES. If it doesn't, circle NO.

1. A state can put a picture of its discoverer, Jedediah Smith, on every 50-dollar bill.

    YES   NO

2. A state can make Elizabeth Cady Stanton's birthday a school holiday.

    YES   NO

3. A state can set a speed limit of 45 miles per hour on a state road.

    YES   NO

4. A state can pass a law that all motorcycle riders must wear helmets.

    YES   NO

5. A state can stop out-of-state businesses from shipping their goods through the state.

    YES   NO

6. A state can add 30 days to the school year.

    YES   NO

7. A state can raise taxes to get money for new roads.

    YES   NO

8. A state can keep farmers from selling their crops to people in other states.

    YES   NO

9. A state can set up its own court system.

    YES   NO

10. A state can limit certain freedoms in order to protect the public's well-being.

    YES   NO

Chapter 7

RUNNING THE STATES

Words to Know

attorney general   the chief lawyer of a state; the federal government also has an attorney general

elections   the process of choosing people for government offices by voting

governor   the leader of the executive branch of a state government

lieutenant governor   the person next in line for the governor's job if the governor quits, gets sick, or dies

officials   people who hold government offices

secretary of state   the person in state government who keeps state records and who runs state elections

superintendent of schools   in some states, the person who heads the state public schools

Has your state ever been hit by a terrible storm, such as a blizzard, a tornado, or a hurricane? Have you ever felt an earthquake, watched a smoking volcano, or seen a flood or a forest fire? These things do not always cause a lot of damage. But sometimes they do. When that happens, the state government steps in to help.

When a state is hit by something beyond its control, the **governor** may fly to the trouble spot. Maybe thousands of people are hurt or homeless. Maybe telephone and power lines are down. Maybe there isn't enough food or there aren't enough hospital beds. The governor goes to see how much damage there is and to decide what the state government can do to help. When the governor flies back to the state capital, he or she meets with **officials** from the state government. And usually that same day, the governor goes on television to promise help for the battered cities and towns. By the next morning, the state is sending food, clothing, doctors, or other help where it is needed.

Not everything a governor does is so important. But whenever state government is in the news, you'll probably see the governor —greeting important visitors, talking to lawmakers, making speeches on television, visiting parts of the state. As the head of the state executive branch, the governor is the most important person in state government. To most people, the governor stands for state government and all the things it does.

Every state has its own laws about who can be governor. But all states agree on three things. A governor must:

- have been born a United States citizen or have become one
- have lived in the state for some time (usually five years)
- be a certain age to run for office (30 years old in most states)

In most states, governors serve a four-year term. People in these states believe that a governor needs four years to do what he or she was elected to do. But in Arkansas, New Hampshire, Vermont, and Rhode Island, a governor serves only two years. These states believe that short terms help keep their governors in close touch with the needs of the people. If the governor doesn't do what the people want, in two years or less the people can vote for a new governor.

The State Governor

A state is almost like a country within a country. And running a state government is very much like running the federal government. So the governor, as head of the state executive branch, has many of the same jobs as the president of the United States.

Chief Executive The governor has a general power to see that laws are carried out. This power gives the governor a lot of control over what happens in the state.

For one thing, the governor has some control over the state's money. It is the governor who draws up the state budget—the plan for spending the state's money. But this budget must be passed by the legislative branch. That branch may change some parts of the budget. But the governor and the legislature usually try to work together on such important matters as the budget.

The governor also has control over state departments, which take care of things like health, farming, highways, jails, state parks, and schools. The governor makes the budget for each of these departments. So the departments can do only those things that the governor has put in the budget. The highway department, for example, can't take money meant for road repairs and use it to build a new bridge.

The Jobs of the Governor

Do You Know?

One governor of Texas, Pappy O'Daniel, started out selling flour on the radio, backed by a country band. His listeners talked him into running for governor. And he kept his radio show after he was elected.

As chief executive, the governor also has the power to choose some of the people who run the state departments. And, of course, the governor chooses people who agree with him or her on what needs to be done and how to do it. So these department heads usually will run their departments the way the governor wants.

Chief of State As a state leader, the governor must make speeches, greet visitors, and appear at special gatherings that are important to the state.

Chief Diplomat The governor often holds talks with other governors and with people from the federal government. In these meetings, the governor represents the people of the state.

Chief Lawmaker The governor can't make laws directly; only the legislative branch can. But the governor has the power to veto bills. And if the governor works for a bill, it often has a good chance of being passed and becoming a law.

Party Chief The governor is the leader of the party he or she belongs to—the Democratic party, the Republican party, or some other party. Usually the governor works closely with other state party members and helps them.

Governor Mark White of Texas and Houston Mayor Kathy Whitmire make an aerial tour of the destruction left by hurricane Alicia in 1983.

Even Alaska, the state with the fewest people, has almost half a million people. And no one person can run a government that has to meet the needs of that many people. So every governor depends on a team for help. And this team usually has some of the following people on it.

- *Lieutenant Governor.* Forty-three states have a **lieutenant governor** who leads state senate meetings. This person becomes governor if the elected governor quits, gets very sick, or dies.

- *Attorney General.* Every state has an **attorney general** who serves as the state's head lawyer in important trials. The attorney general also decides whether things the state wants to do are legal.

- *Secretary of State.* Every state has a **secretary of state**. This person keeps all the official records of the state. The secretary of state also must run all state **elections** and make sure that they are fair and legal.

- *Superintendent of Public Instruction.* Most states have a **superintendent of public instruction** who runs the state's public schools. This person helps decide what subjects are taught in school and what special classes are needed.

The Governor's Team

The different state departments make up the largest part of the governor's team. Every state has departments that control such things as highways, jails, farming, health, and state parks. Some special departments work with businesses, such as mining or banking. Some control state libraries. Others test doctors and lawyers before they are allowed to work in the state. Still others set rules for clean air or for safety on the job. Together these departments take care of a lot of the day-to-day government work for the governor.

State Departments

The Governor and the President

Some people think that the job of governor is good training for the job of president. In many ways, the two jobs are alike. But they are different in three important ways.

First, a governor's power is limited to just one state. The governor has no control over what happens in any other state. But the president has power over all the states. He makes decisions for the country as a whole, not just for one state.

Second, the governor has no control over the army, navy, or air force. As commander-in-chief, the president controls the country's armed forces.

Third, the governor must share his or her executive power with some other elected officials. In many states, the lieutenant governor, attorney general, secretary of state, superintendent of public instruction, and others are elected by the people. In such cases, the governor can't fire these officials or directly control them. But the president doesn't have to share executive power with anyone. All the main people in the executive branch, except the vice president, are put in office by the president. So the president has direct control over these officials and can remove them at any time.

But even with these three differences, the governor's job is much like the president's job. Both the governor and the president are leaders of the executive branches of their governments. Both have the jobs of chief executive, chief diplomat, chief lawmaker, and party chief. The governor chooses some of the heads of the state departments, just as the president chooses the heads of the cabinet departments. Both the governor and the president draw up budgets for spending government money. Both have the power to veto bills passed by their legislative branches. And, of course, both the governor and the president have the important job of following the will of the people.

Since the jobs are so much alike, it is no surprise that some governors have gone on to become presidents. Out of 40 presidents, 16 were once governors. This shows that the job of running a state really can lead to the job of running a country.

Exercise 7

Read each sentence below and decide whether it describes the job of the PRESIDENT, a GOVERNOR, or BOTH. Then circle the right answer.

1. This person lets departments take care of much of the day-to-day government work.

    PRESIDENT   GOVERNOR   BOTH

2. This person's secretary of state may be elected by the people.

    PRESIDENT   GOVERNOR   BOTH

3. This person may be elected for two years.

    PRESIDENT   GOVERNOR   BOTH

4. This person serves as chief of state by making speeches and greeting visitors.

    PRESIDENT   GOVERNOR   BOTH

5. This person must draw up a budget to send to the legislative branch.

    PRESIDENT   GOVERNOR   BOTH

6. This person is commander-in-chief of all the country's armed forces.

    PRESIDENT   GOVERNOR   BOTH

7. This person can veto bills passed by the legislative branch.

    PRESIDENT   GOVERNOR   BOTH

8. This person must share executive power with other elected officials.

    PRESIDENT   GOVERNOR   BOTH

9. This person makes decisions for the whole country.

    PRESIDENT   GOVERNOR   BOTH

Chapter 8

MAKING STATE LAWS

Words to Know

district a part of a state that elects one state representative or one state senator

initiative a way for the people of a state to pass a law; if enough people sign an initiative, the state must hold an election to let the people vote on it

petition a written notice signed by many people telling the state government to take some action; initiatives, referendums, and recalls are three kinds of petitions

recall a way for the people to remove a state senator or state representative from office; if enough people sign the recall notice, the state must let everyone vote to decide whether the person should be removed from office

referendum a way for the people to stop the state legislature from passing a bill; if enough people sign the referendum, the state must let everyone vote to decide whether the law should be passed

state legislature the legislative, or lawmaking, branch of the state government

If you're ever in the capital city of your state, you'll have the chance to see your state legislative branch in action. You can visit the big rooms where the members of the state legislative branch meet. In these rooms are the raised stands where the leaders of the legislative branch give speeches and the many rows of desks where the members sit. The members themselves will be at work, listening to speakers, making speeches of their own, and voting on bills.

But that's not the only place you can see members of the state legislative branch at work. Your own members—the ones you elect—have offices near you. And when they're not meeting in the state capital, they're back in your part of the state, where they spend a good part of the year.

You might see the members who represent you in person, in the newspaper, or on television. You might see them at a fair or at the opening of a new bridge. They speak to clubs and citizens' groups and meet with business people. Sometimes they visit farms and factories and talk to shoppers on the city streets. All these things are part of their job.

To do a good job, your members in the state legislative branch have to do more than just make speeches. They have to keep in touch with you and your neighbors. And they have to know what's going on in your part of the state. Only then can they pass laws that will help the people they represent.

Each year, members of the **state legislature** come from all parts of the state to the state's capital city. For months, they hold daily meetings in the state capitol building. The members work on new state laws and decide how the state should be run.

Most states call their legislative branch the state legislature. Some call it the general assembly, the legislative assembly, or the general court. No matter what it's called, almost every state legislative branch has two houses—a lower house and an upper house. Only Nebraska doesn't; it has only one house—the senate.

The Lower House A state legislature's lower house is the larger of the two houses and is usually called the house of representatives. Each state is split into **districts**. Each district has about the same number of people in it. And each district elects one state representative. Alaska has 40 state representatives, each representing about 10,000 people. New Hampshire has 400 state representatives, each representing about 20,000 people.

Most state representatives serve two-year terms. Because most state legislatures meet during only a few months of the year, most representatives work part-time for the government. They usually have other jobs just like other citizens for most of the year. That's why a state's lower house is often called the "people's house." State representatives are often the people closest to the voters.

The Upper House The upper house in every state is called the state senate. The state senate always has fewer members than the lower house, and they usually serve four-year terms.

Members of the state senate, called state senators, are elected from districts within the state, just as state representatives are. And each senator in the state represents just about the same number of people. Alaska has 20 state senators, each representing about 20,000 people. Minnesota has 67 state senators, each representing about 60,000 people.

Like the state representatives, most state senators work only part-time. Few states pay state senators to work all year.

The State Legislature

Passing State Laws

In many ways, the state legislatures are patterned after the United States Congress. Except for Nebraska, each state has a two-house system just like Congress. And state legislatures make laws the same way Congress does. They follow the same six steps.

1. A state representative or a state senator writes a bill.

2. The bill is passed by a committee in the house where it began.

3. The bill is passed by a majority of members in the house where it began.

4. The bill is passed by a committee and then by a majority of members in the other house.

5. A special committee works out any differences in the bills passed by each house. Then the bill is passed again by both houses.

6. The governor can sign the bill into law or veto it. If the bill is vetoed, it must pass again in each house with a 2/3 majority to become a law.

New Jersey State Representative Christopher Jackman arrives at the House with his hands full of bills to be studied by the legislature.

How much power do people really have over the laws that get passed? Of course, the people themselves elect the lawmakers in both the Congress and the state legislature. And they try to vote for the men and women who will pass laws that will help them. But in state government, the people's power doesn't stop there.

Suppose the people of a state want a new law or want to stop a bill from becoming a law. Or suppose the people want to remove a senator or a representative from office because he or she is doing a bad job. In many states, there are three ways that the people can take direct action.

Initiative About half of the states allow people to use an **initiative** to make new laws. The people who want a new law write it down and sign their names. Then they try to get other people to sign the **petition**. If enough people sign it, the voters decide in an election whether the initiative should become a law.

Referendum About half of the states allow people to use a **referendum** to stop a bill that their state legislature is trying to pass. The people who want to stop the bill sign their names to the referendum petition. If enough people sign it, the bill is taken out of the hands of the state legislature. Then the people themselves vote on the bill. If the majority votes against the bill, it doesn't become a law. The people can even use a referendum on a bill that has already been passed by the state legislature, as long as it hasn't gone into action yet.

Recall About one-fourth of the states allow people to use a **recall**. By using a recall, the people can remove an elected state official from office before his or her term is finished. People who want to remove a state senator, for example, sign their names to the recall petition. If enough people sign the recall, a new election for the senator's job must be held within a short time. The senator must run for election all over again against other people who want the job. The person who gets the majority vote in this recall election becomes the state senator.

The People's Power

How Massachusetts Got a New Law

A bill can take many paths on its way to becoming a state law. Most state laws are just passed by the state legislature in one round. But sometimes a bill is vetoed by the governor and must be passed by the legislature again. And once in a while, the people of the state vote on a bill through an initiative or referendum. Almost never does a bill follow *all* these paths to become a law. But that's just what happened with Massachusetts's "bottle law."

A bottle law states that companies cannot sell certain foods or drinks in no-return bottles that people just throw away. Instead, the products must come in bottles that people can return to supermarkets and other stores. People get money for the bottles they bring back, and the companies can use the bottles over again. The law is supposed to cut down on roadside litter. And it is supposed to help stop the waste of making so many new bottles.

In 1978 the Massachusetts Bottle Bill was debated before the state legislature's Energy Committee, led by Representative Lois G. Pines, a sponsor of the bill.

Oregon had the first bottle law in 1972. And when people saw that the Oregon law seemed to be working, other states got interested. By 1979, many people in Massachusetts wanted to have a bottle law for their state. One of these people was Representative Lois Pines of the state legislature. She started a bottle bill in the Massachusetts House of Representatives. By September 1980, the bill had passed both the House and the Senate. It seemed ready to become a law.

But the governor of Massachusetts, Edward King, didn't want a bottle law. He thought it would cause too much work for store owners. Then the store owners would raise their prices to cover the cost of this extra work. So Governor King vetoed the bill and sent it back to the state legislature. Even after the veto, the bill was still popular. So by November of 1981, the state legislature passed the bill again over the governor's veto. It was set to become a law at the beginning of 1983.

But there were still people who didn't want any bottle law. They were joined by bottling companies that felt the law would cost them too much money. They wanted an election so that the people of Massachusetts could say directly whether they wanted the law. So they started a referendum and got more than 29,000 people to sign it. The referendum forced the state government to let people vote on the bottle law in the next election.

Before the election, citizens' groups and members of the state legislature spoke for both sides. But in November 1982, when the election finally came, it was time for the people of Massachusetts to speak. And they voted by a big majority to pass the bottle law. So in January 1983, the new law went into action.

It took three years to make the Massachusetts bottle law. But in the end, the majority of people in Massachusetts got the law they wanted. In state government, as in federal government, the people have the final say.

Exercise 8

Read each sentence below and decide whether it describes a STATE legislature, the FEDERAL legislature, or BOTH. Then circle the right answer.

1. A committee must pass a bill before the full house votes on it.

    STATE   FEDERAL   BOTH

2. The people can use a recall to remove members of either house.

    STATE   FEDERAL   BOTH

3. By using an initiative, the people can force the legislature to let them vote on a law.

    STATE   FEDERAL   BOTH

4. All members of the upper house are elected from districts, just as members of the lower house are.

    STATE   FEDERAL   BOTH

5. Members of the legislature do government work full time during the year.

    STATE   FEDERAL   BOTH

6. The people can use a referendum to stop a law that has already been passed by the legislature but has not yet gone into action.

    STATE   FEDERAL   BOTH

7. Most of the time, both houses must pass a bill and the head of the executive branch must sign it before it becomes a law.

    STATE   FEDERAL   BOTH

8. If the head of the executive branch vetoes a bill, the legislature can try to pass it again over the veto.

    STATE   FEDERAL   BOTH

9. There are more members in the lower house than in the upper house.

    STATE   FEDERAL   BOTH

Chapter 9

GOING THROUGH STATE COURTS

Words to Know

civil cases   cases usually between a person and a business over a money matter, such as an unpaid bill

criminal cases   cases in which someone has broken a law; such crimes as robbery and murder are criminal cases

innocent   not guilty; having done nothing against the law

witnesses   people who have seen, heard, or know things that are important to a case and who are called upon to tell these things in court

Y̶ou've probably seen many trials on television. You've seen the judge wearing a long black robe. You've seen the lawyers asking sharp questions and the person on trial looking worried. And you've seen the jury—listening, watching, trying to decide whether the person on trial is guilty.

The courts in most television trials are state courts. State courts decide cases of robbery or murder or hit-and-run driving. And state courts are where most jury trials take place.

Someday you'll probably see a real state court trial—from the jury box. Like most people, you have a good chance of being called to serve on a jury at least once in your life. And if you are called it will be your job to help decide whether the person on trial is guilty or not guilty.

But why do the courts need juries? And why do they want all different kinds of people to make decisions instead of people with legal training, such as a judges or lawyers?

People on trial can lose a lot—their freedom, their money, their good name. So the people who set up our court system tried to make sure that the trials would be fair. They knew that one person, even a trained person, can make mistakes. But a whole group of people are less likely to make mistakes. It takes a strong case to make a group of all different kinds of people agree that someone is guilty of a crime. If the case leaves so many questions that a jury of people from all parts of the community can't agree, then the case is too weak to take away a person's freedom.

Partly because of juries, our courts often move very slowly. It can take months before a trial is finally over. And sometimes a jury can take weeks to make its decision. But the jury system is one way to make sure that trials are fair and that people who are not guilty are protected.

The State Court System

The state judicial branch is set up very much like the federal judicial branch. It also has three kinds of courts. The lowest state courts are the general trial courts. These are the courts that have juries. Most state cases begin here. The next higher courts are the state courts of appeals. There are no juries in these courts, only groups of judges. They can review decisions of the general trial courts. The highest state court is the state supreme court. This court can review decisions of both lower courts and has the last word on the meaning of the state constitution. Sometimes state supreme court decisions can be reviewed by the United States Supreme Court. This happens only when a state supreme court's decision raises a question about federal law or the United States Constitution.

Together the three state courts handle cases that deal with state laws. They handle three main kinds of cases:

- *Cases dealing with the state constitution.* State courts take cases that question what the state constitution and state laws mean.

- *Criminal cases dealing with state laws.* **Criminal cases** are cases in which someone has broken a law. Such crimes as robbery, murder, or drunk driving are against state law and are handled in state courts.

- *Civil cases within one state.* **Civil cases** usually have to do with arguments between people or businesses over money. Cases of unpaid bills or broken promises are civil cases. If both people or businesses in a civil case are from the same state, the case goes to state court.

General Trial Courts

Every state is split into state judicial districts. And each district has its own general trial court. Some large states have many of these courts, such as Ohio, which has 88 general trial courts. But Rhode Island, a small state, has only four.

These courts handle cases in the same way—with one judge and a jury. The judge must make sure that the trial is fair and that it follows the rules. The judge decides what facts can be presented and what questions the lawyers can't ask. And the judge usually sets the sentence if someone is found guilty.

The jury must decide who is guilty and who is **innocent**, who is right and who is wrong. Usually the jury is made up of 12 people who live in the judicial district. In some states, the jury may have as few as six people for less important cases.

The State and Federal Court Systems

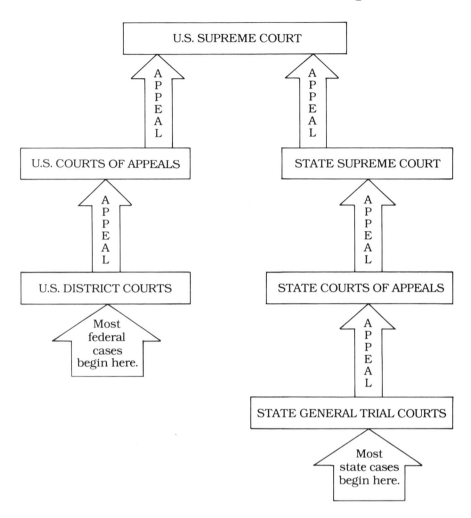

The people on the jury listen to all the facts of the case, to the **witnesses**, and to the lawyers from both sides. In a criminal case, they must decide whether a person is guilty or not guilty. In a civil case, they must decide whether anyone has done wrong, and if so, how that person must repay the wrong. In most cases, *all* the jury members must agree on the decision. If they can't all agree, another trial is held and another jury is chosen.

Do juries always make the right decisions? Are trials always run fairly, by the rules? Some people don't think so. Sometimes the person found guilty by a general trial court thinks the trial was unfair. When this happens, the person can appeal to a higher court.

The State Courts of Appeals

In many states, the case goes to a state court of appeals. This court has no jury, only a judge. The judge doesn't hold a new trial, and most of the time, the judge doesn't question the facts that were presented in the general trial court.

Instead, the court of appeals must decide whether the trial in the lower court was fair. If anyone made mistakes in the trial, the judge can change the lower court's decision or order a new trial. If not, the judge will let the first decision stand. Usually the court of appeals makes the final decision.

The State Supreme Court

Is it possible for both a general trial court and a court of appeals to make a wrong decision? Some people think it can happen. For them, the state supreme court is usually the last chance to get a court decision changed.

But most cases never reach the state supreme court. Out of thousands of cases handled by the lower courts, only a few are ever appealed to the state's highest court. And even then, the court can decide not to take a case if there is no good reason for the appeal.

Even so, most state supreme courts decide a hundred or more cases each year. Some of these cases have to do with the meaning of state laws or the state constitution. But most are cases that have been appealed from the lower state courts.

The state supreme court handles appeal cases in much the same way as the state courts of appeals. The court doesn't hold a new trial and doesn't have a jury. Instead, the court goes over the case records to make sure that the trial was fair and that the law was followed. Unlike the appeals courts, the final decision is made by, not one, but several judges. These judges, called justices, decide whether to let the lower court's decision stand, to change the decision, or to order a new trial.

The state supreme court justices have the last word in almost every appeal case and every case about the meaning of the state laws and constitution. But sometimes a case can move from the state supreme court to the United States Supreme Court. If a case brings up any question about federal laws or the United States Constitution, the United States Supreme Court can review the state supreme court's decision.

31579

2222222222222222222

A Case That Changed the Law

All three state courts work together to make sure that everyone is treated fairly under the law. To be fair, the courts use state laws to make their decision. But are the state laws themselves always fair to everyone? The United State Supreme Court justices sometimes decide that they're not, as they did in the case of Clarence Gideon.

The trial of Clarence Gideon started on August 4, 1961, in a Florida general trial court—the Circuit Court of Bay County. Gideon was on trial for robbing a poolroom at about 5:30 A.M. on June 3, 1961. Police said he stole money and took some beer and wine. Gideon could get a five-year sentence for this crime.

When Gideon first appeared in court, the judge asked whether he was ready. Gideon said no, he didn't have a lawyer because he didn't have any money. He wanted the court to get a free lawyer for him. But the laws of Florida and other states said that the court didn't have to give the person on trial a free lawyer in cases like Gideon's. And the judge in Gideon's case decided there was no special reason why Gideon should have a free lawyer.

So Gideon had to act as his own lawyer. The judge tried to help during the trial. He asked Gideon whether he wanted any new jury members, told him how to talk to the jury, and warned the jury to be fair.

Clarence Gideon took his case all the way to the Supreme Court. And because he did, a law was passed to assure a fair trial for people who cannot afford to hire their own lawyers.

Do You Know?

Abe Fortas, the lawyer who represented Clarence Gideon before the United States Supreme Court, later became a Supreme Court justice himself.

But even with the judge's help, the jury found Gideon guilty. They believed a witness who said he had seen Gideon come out of the poolroom at 5:30 A.M. with a bottle of wine. Gideon was sentenced to five years in jail.

Gideon wrote to the United States Supreme Court and asked to have the decision overturned. He felt that it was against the United States Constitution for Florida to put him on trial without a lawyer. The Supreme Court agreed to take his case.

Gideon himself didn't appear before the Supreme Court. Instead, the Court gave him a well-known lawyer named Abe Fortas to represent him. Fortas pointed out to the Supreme Court that the United States Constitution promises everyone a fair trial. But Gideon didn't get a fair trial because he couldn't have a lawyer. And he couldn't have a lawyer because he couldn't pay for one. So, Fortas said, Florida's law went against the Constitution by not allowing Gideon to have a free lawyer.

The Supreme Court agreed. The Court ruled that all states had to get a free lawyer for any person who couldn't pay for one. And it ordered Florida to give Gideon a new trial with a lawyer to represent him.

On July 5, 1962, Gideon was back in court. But this time he had a lawyer, Fred Turner. As before, the case against Gideon depended on the witness who said he had seen Gideon coming out of the poolroom at 5:30 in the morning. But Turner asked the witness questions and showed how his story might not be true. And Turner showed that the witness himself could have robbed the poolroom. This time the jury decided that Gideon was not guilty.

Gideon's case took almost a year to go through the court system. But because Gideon appealed to the Supreme Court, he got a new trial and was found innocent. And because Gideon appealed, the Supreme Court found that Florida's law—and other state laws like it—went against the Constitution. So the Court forced the states to give up these laws. Now everyone has a better chance of getting a fair trial.

Exercise 9

Read each sentence below and decide which court it describes. Then circle the letter of the right answer.

1. This court would be the first to handle a robbery trial.

   (a) state supreme court

   (b) state court of appeals

   (c) state general trial court

2. This court can take appeals from the first trial court.

   (a) state court of appeals

   (b) state supreme court

   (c) both of the above

3. This court can take an appeal from a state supreme court.

   (a) state court of appeals

   (b) United States Supreme Court

   (c) none of the above

4. This court would be the first to take a civil case between people from the same state.

   (a) state general trial court

   (b) state court of appeals

   (c) state supreme court

5. In this court, decisions can be made by a jury.

   (a) state court of appeals

   (b) state general trial court

   (c) state supreme court

6. This court has the last word on the meaning of the state constitution.

   (a) state court of appeals

   (b) state supreme court

   (c) state general trial court

YOUR LOCAL GOVERNMENT

Chapter 10

RUNNING COUNTY AND CITY GOVERNMENTS

Words to Know

assessor a local government official who decides how much tax people must pay on such things as land, houses, and buildings that they own

city council a small group of people elected by the people of a city to make laws and run the city government

city manager a person hired by a city government to work as the city's chief executive

commission a small group of people elected by the people of a city to make laws for the city and to run city government; each person on a commission is also the head of a local department

commissioner a member of a commission

community groups groups run by local people, not the government, to help people in need

community services office an office that helps people find out what services they can get from county, city, or town government

county board a small group of people elected by the people of a county to make laws for the county and to run county government

mayor the person who is elected head of a city council

sheriff the head of the county law officers; the sheriff makes sure that people follow the county laws

No matter where you live, there are people in government working for you. There are people in federal government who work for the good of *all* Americans—more than 226 million of us! And there are people in each state government who work for the people living in all parts of the state. In Alaska, the state government works for the half a million people who live there. The California government works for the state's 24 million people.

But because federal and state governments must work for so many people, they can handle only matters that are important to very large groups of people. But what about matters that are important only to small groups of people? The federal and state governments do not have time to listen to the problems of one small town or city. That's why every town, city, and county in the country has a local government.

A local government will never stop a war between countries, send people to the moon, or build a 1,000-mile highway. But often the things it does can make a big difference in your everyday life.

Local government takes care of small things—things close to home. And usually these are the things that are most important to you. Are the streets in your town safe to drive on? Is there a hospital nearby if you need one? Are there police officers and fire fighters you can call if you're in trouble? Your local government handles these things and many more. In many ways, your local government affects your everyday life more than any other level of government.

How Local Government Is Set Up

Across the United States, millions of people live in towns and cities of all sizes. And there are millions more people who don't live in a town at all, who live miles from their nearest neighbors. So it's not surprising that there are different kinds of local government.

One kind of local government is the county government. Every state is split into counties, sometimes called parishes or divisions. Some small states have only a few counties, such as Delaware, which has three. But most states have many more. Texas has the most—254 counties in all. Some counties, such as Denver in Colorado, cover just one big city and nothing else. Others, such as Inyo County in California, are mostly open land and mountains with hardly any towns at all. But usually counties have a number of cities and towns inside the county lines, as well as farms, ranches, and other land.

Another kind of local government is city government. There are about 19,000 different cities and towns across the United States. A city that has more than a million people can't be run the same way as a town of 1,500. And a town in the desert of New Mexico will have different problems than a town in the rainy mountains of Washington. So they each have their own local government.

Since almost all cities and towns are inside counties, the people who live in them have two local governments—the city and the county. These two governments work together to meet the needs of the people.

In many ways, local governments are like the federal and state governments. They, too, have their own written laws, and leaders elected by the people. And they, too, have three jobs to do—executive, legislative, and judicial. But there is one important difference. In local government, the executive and legislative branches are run by the same people. So the people who make the laws also make sure that the laws are carried out.

County Government

The day-to-day work of running a county takes place in a town or city called the county seat. There the **county board** meets to try to solve the county's problems. Most county boards have between five and nine members elected by the people of the county. The board's job is to run the county and make its laws. Among other things, the board has the power to set taxes and decide how the money should be spent. And it works together with different county departments and the people who run them.

There are many officials who help the county board, and often they also are elected by the people. For example, the county **sheriff** makes sure that people follow the county laws. The county **assessor** decides how much tax people must pay on the land they own. And the county clerk records births, deaths, and marriages in the county.

City Government

Is there a city hall or town hall near where you live? In this building, the city government makes laws, carries them out, and upholds them in court. Different cities set up their governments in different ways. But they use one of three plans.

City Council-Mayor In most American cities, the people of the city elect a **city council**, made up of five to nine council members, and a **mayor**. Together the council and the mayor make up the legislative and executive branches of the city government.

In some cities, the city council has most of the power. It passes laws, makes the city budget, and hires and fires other city officials. In these cities, the mayor may have a few extra jobs, such as leading council meetings. But mostly the mayor just acts as one more council member.

Diane Feinstein, mayor of San Francisco, CA, meets with members of the press in her office.

But in many large cities, the mayor has more power than any council member. In these cities, they mayor is a real chief executive. He or she can veto laws passed by the council, make up the city budget, and often choose many city department heads.

City Council-City Manager This kind of city government also has a city council, and sometimes a mayor, elected by the people. But under this plan, the city council hires a **city manager** to take over most of the chief executive's job. The city manager runs the day-to-day business of the city and usually is especially trained for this job.

Commission A **commission** is made up of **commissioners** elected by the people of the city. These commissioners have much the same power that the city council members do. But here, each commissioner is in charge of one or more city departments. This kind of city government is often used in small cities and towns.

Local Departments

Even the smallest counties or towns have problems to solve, needs to meet, and people to help. It's a big job, and the leaders of a local government cannot do all the work themselves. So they have departments to help them, just as the state and federal governments do.

Just about every local government has a police or sheriff's department and a fire department. Together these departments protect the safety of the people in the city or county. Some of the other departments that local governments may operate to help citizens are:

- *A health department* runs local hospitals. It also makes sure that local restaurants are clean and that the water is safe to drink.

- *A street department* keeps streets and street lights in good repair.

- *A parks department* runs local public parks, playgrounds, swimming pools, beaches, lakes, and other recreational places.

The job of local government is to run the county, city, or town to meet the needs of all local people—you and your neighbors. Much of the work is done by local departments that take care of things the whole town or city needs. But who takes care of the special needs and problems that just a few people have? What about the people who are sick and can't pay for a doctor? Or older people who have no family or friends and no place to go? Local government is there to help them too.

Most local governments have a **community services office** that can help people with special needs and problems. The workers are trained to answer people's questions, and they know what government can do to help. Here are some of the services many local governments pay for:

- *Low-cost health care.* Most counties have a public health center where people can get low-cost medical care.

- *Help for older people.* Many local governments run centers where older people can meet, find new friends, and have a good time. In some places, older people pay less to use public buses and can get low-cost meals.

- *Schooling for adults.* Many local schools have night classes for adults who did not finish high school. Sometimes there are classes for people who do not speak or read English well.

There are many other services that local governments provide, but even so, no local government can meet all local needs. That's why there are also school groups, church groups, and other **community groups**, such as the American Red Cross and the Salvation Army, to help people in need. Working together, local government and community groups do their best to make your community a better place to live.

Local Government Services and Community Groups

The American Red Cross gives food, housing, and medical care to people who are victims of disasters such as floods, hurricanes, and earthquakes.

Exercise 10

Decide whether each sentence below describes local government. If it does, circle TRUE. If not, circle FALSE.

1. A mayor of a town or city is elected by the people.
   TRUE   FALSE

2. Only groups of people can get help from local government.
   TRUE   FALSE

3. A city government may have a chief executive who is hired by the government, not elected by the people.
   TRUE   FALSE

4. The legislative and judicial branches of local government are run by the same people.
   TRUE   FALSE

5. The mayor of a city always has a lot more power than a city council member.
   TRUE   FALSE

6. A county board is usually run by a city manager.
   TRUE   FALSE

7. City council members are usually chosen by the manager.
   TRUE   FALSE

8. The local government of small towns and cities is often run by commissioners.
   TRUE   FALSE

9. Many county governments help pay for public health centers where people can get low-cost medical care.
   TRUE   FALSE

10. The heads of local departments are always elected by the people themselves.
    TRUE   FALSE

Chapter 11

MAKING LOCAL LAWS

Words to Know

disturbing the peace breaking local laws by making noise or acting in ways that bother other people

property things that someone owns, such as land or buildings

trespassing entering people's houses or buildings or going onto their land without permission

vandalism harming or destroying things that someone else owns

In a town in Georgia, it's against the law for a chicken to cross any road inside the town limits. And in a city in Indiana, it's against the law to carry a watermelon into a public park.

It's hard to think just what the people who made these local laws had in mind. You might even be able to find some laws in your own city or county that are just as strange as these. You would at least find many local laws that are special just to your city or county. And these laws, even the strange ones, are made to do one thing—to protect people's rights.

Sometimes local laws seem to take away people's rights. Laws usually tell people what they can't do, not what they can do. But laws put limits on the rights of some people to protect the more important rights of all people. So building laws may take away someone's right to put up any kind of building that person wants. But these laws protect everyone from buildings that are badly made and unsafe. And a noise law may take away someone's right to have loud parties late at night. But it protects the rights of the people in the neighborhood to get a good night's sleep.

Sometimes you'll find laws that keep you from doing something you want to do. But these laws will probably give you back much more than they take away from you.

Kinds of Local Laws

Whether you live in a big city or miles from the nearest town, there are local laws to follow. Some local laws are more important than others, but almost all of them are made either to protect people or to protect **property**.

Some laws protect people from being hurt. There are laws against keeping dangerous animals that might attack people. Other laws set speed limits and control traffic to cut down car accidents. And still other laws tell how many people a room or an elevator can safely hold.

There are laws to stop people from doing things in public that bother other people. For example, most towns have laws against being drunk in public and against begging. And every place has laws against **disturbing the peace**—bothering other people with noisy parties, loud music late at night, fights, and other things.

Laws also protect people's property. There are **trespassing** laws to keep people from entering someone's house, office, or land without permission. There are **vandalism** laws to keep people from harming things that belong to someone else. And most towns have other laws that protect buildings and property owned by the local government.

Making Local Laws

The members of a county board or city council have an important job—making laws for their county, town, or city. The laws they make change the way hundreds, thousands, or even millions of people do things. That's why local lawmakers are chosen by the people themselves to do this job. Because they are elected, lawmakers are more likely to make laws that are good for the people.

Ideas for new local laws are usually brought up by a board member or council member during a meeting. The other members think it over, sometimes for weeks. And they ask questions. Is the law really necessary? How much will it cost? Will the law take away more rights than it protects? Finally the council or board members vote on the law. Sometimes the mayor or chief executive can veto a new law. But if enough members want the law, it will pass.

Taking Part in Local Government

Do you have an idea for a law to make life better? Maybe you want a lower speed limit on your street so that children will be safer when they walk to school. Or maybe you want stronger laws to cut down on street crime. Whatever the idea, there are five things all local citizens can do to get the laws they want.

1. They can vote for council members who agree with them. If people elect a good council, they're likely to have good laws.

2. They can talk to the council member who represents them. This person usually lives nearby and knows their neighborhood. But people have to tell their council member what they need.

3. They can go to the council meetings where new laws are made. Sometimes local citizens can speak to the council, explaining why they think a law should or should not be passed. These people can't vote because they aren't council members. But what they say can change how the council members vote.

4. They can use petitions. Some petitions—such as recalls, initiatives, and referendums—have legal power. People can use them to change laws or to get rid of council members that they think are doing poor jobs. Other petitions don't have legal power. They only *ask* the council to do something. But the council members will think carefully about a petition that is signed by many people.

People who take part in their local government have the power to make it work for them. They can change old laws and work for new ones. The people's power is stronger in local government than at any other level of government.

The people who live in the towns of America can get together and talk about the laws they would like to see passed.

Exercise 11

Decide how to finish each sentence below so that it describes local laws and local lawmaking. Then circle the letter of the best answer.

1. When a city council is talking over a new law, local citizens usually can

   (a) listen to the council and speak for their own points of view.

   (b) listen to the council and then vote on the law.

   (c) not change what the council does in any way.

2. People can use petitions to change

   (a) only local laws.

   (b) only state laws.

   (c) both state and local laws.

3. Petitions to local governments that are signed by many people

   (a) always have legal power.

   (b) sometimes have legal power.

   (c) never have legal power.

4. Someone who quietly camped out in another person's backyard without permission would be guilty of

   (a) disturbing the peace.

   (b) vandalism.

   (c) trespassing.

5. Local laws protect

   (a) property from trespassers and vandals.

   (b) people from harm and actions that disturb the peace.

   (c) both property and people.

6. The laws that local lawmakers pass can change the way thousands of people do things. For this reason, local lawmakers

   (a) are elected by the city council or county board.

   (b) are elected by local people.

   (c) are chosen by the mayor.

Chapter 12

GOING THROUGH LOCAL COURTS

Words to Know

bail money paid by people who have been arrested as a promise that they will appear for trial; once bail is paid, the people are released from jail until the trial.

divorce court a local civil court that handles cases of married people who want to break up

justice courts county courts that handle criminal cases

juvenile court a local court that handles cases of people who aren't legally adults

misdemeanors less serious crimes for which the sentence has to be less than one year in a local jail

probate court a local civil court that decides who will get the belongings of a person who has died

small claims court a local civil court that takes only cases about small amounts of money, usually less than $1,000

If it was always easy for everyone to see the truth, there would be no need for courts. Only the person guilty of a crime would be arrested. And two drivers in a car accident would agree on who was to blame.

But most of the time, it's hard to find the truth. A man arrested for robbery may say he is innocent. Each person in a car accident may say the other is at fault. So we have courts to help solve these problems, to help us find the truth.

Courts have tough rules about how trials must be run, what facts can be presented, and how decisions must be made. These rules mean that court cases are often long and difficult for everyone in them. But these tough rules are very important for two reasons:

- They help make sure that the court reaches the right decision.

- They protect the rights of all the people in the case.

But suppose you have just a small problem. A police officer gave you a $25 traffic ticket that you think is unfair. Or a neighbor backed into your car, and you had to pay $200 to get it fixed. Problems like these are not worth a big trial in a state court. But you still feel you've been treated unfairly, and you want your rights protected. What can you do?

You can go to a local court. Local courts deal with the less serious cases that state and federal courts were never meant to handle. Like all courts, they work to find the truth in a case. And they protect your rights and make sure you're treated fairly, even in small cases.

The Local Court System

Every city and county has local courts. These courts are really the lowest courts of the state court system. But they are called local courts because they take cases about local laws and problems. They handle both civil and criminal cases.

Civil cases Often a city or a county has special local courts to handle civil cases—cases in which two people can't agree. A **divorce court** settles cases for married people who break up. A **probate court** makes sure the belongings of a person who has died go to the right people. A **small claims court** settles cases for people who can't agree about small amounts of money or goods.

Criminal cases Local courts hold trials only for **misdemeanors** —less serious crimes for which the sentence can't be more than a year in the local jail. A traffic court handles only cases of broken local traffic laws. A **juvenile court** takes only cases in which the person on trial is not legally an adult. Other city courts handle criminal cases of adults, such as shoplifting or disturbing the peace. Outside the city, courts called **justice courts** or county courts handle these cases.

Small Claims Court

Have you ever been unhappy about something you bought or some work someone did for you? Did you discover that the person or company wasn't willing to solve the problem? In most states, you can take such a case to a small claims court if the money or repairs you want total less than $1,000.

A small claims court handles cases quickly. A person may wait weeks for his or her case to come up. But when it does, it often is over in less than 15 minutes. The cases move quickly because small claims courts have no lawyers and no jury. Instead, the people on each side in the case tell their stories directly to the judge. The judge listens, asking questions, and then decides who is wrong and what that person must pay.

Because people don't lose much time and don't have to pay for lawyers in small claims court, they can take even very small problems there. No one has to give up his or her rights just because a case isn't big enough for a state court.

This police officer is ticketing an illegally parked car. The offender usually has a choice of paying a fine or appearing in court.

Traffic Court

Along with small claims courts, traffic courts are some of the busiest local courts. Every day people get tickets for breaking local traffic laws—for speeding, blocking traffic, or careless driving. Many of these people must then appear in traffic court.

Most traffic court cases have no lawyers and no jury—just the judge, the driver, and the police officer who gave the ticket. The police officer and the driver both tell their stories directly to the judge. The judge asks questions and makes the decision. A driver who is found guilty can appeal, but few do because the usual sentence in traffic court is just a fine. Hiring an appeals lawyer often costs more than paying the fine.

Citizens' Rights

Most people who break laws, such as speeding or disturbing the peace, are not arrested or held by the police. They may just get a ticket and be told to pay a fine. Or they may just be given a date to appear in court before a judge.

But people can be arrested for some misdemeanors, such as vandalism or drunk driving. And if people are arrested and held by the police they have rights to protect them and to make sure they are treated fairly.

People who are arrested have the right to stay silent. They don't have to answer any questions if they don't want to. And they can't be found guilty just because they won't answer questions. The law says people are to be treated as if they are innocent until they are proven guilty in court.

They have the right to be taken quickly before a judge. During this first hearing in court, they must be told what crimes they have been arrested for. And they must have the chance to tell the judge whether they are innocent or guilty.

Also at this first hearing, the judge must set an amount of money for bail—the smaller the crime, the lower the bail. People who pay the bail must be released until their trial begins. People out on bail who don't show up for trial lose their bail money. So the bail money acts as a promise that people will appear for trial and not run away.

People who are arrested also have the right to get a lawyer to defend them both before and during the trial. And if a person doesn't have enough money for a lawyer, he or she must be given one for free.

These rights are the very same ones promised to people who face trial in state or federal courts. In local courts, the crimes and the sentences are less serious than those in state and federal courts. But a person's right to a fair trial is just as important and is protected just as strongly, no matter how small the case is.

A lawyer discusses a case to be brought to trial with his client.

Exercise 12

Decide if each sentence below describes local courts. If it does, circle TRUE. If not, circle FALSE.

1. Local courts are part of the state court system.

    TRUE   FALSE

2. Local courts handle civil cases but not criminal cases.

    TRUE   FALSE

3. Misdemeanor cases are usually handled in local courts.

    TRUE   FALSE

4. There are no jury trials in small claims court.

    TRUE   FALSE

5. People have a right to a free lawyer in small claims court.

    TRUE   FALSE

6. People who are arrested and held for trial in local courts have the right to a lawyer, just as in state and federal courts.

    TRUE   FALSE

7. People who are arrested and held for trial in local courts don't have the right to have bail set.

    TRUE   FALSE

8. Local court decisions can never be appealed.

    TRUE   FALSE

9. Most traffic court cases have a judge but no jury.

    TRUE   FALSE

10. People can't be arrested for misdemeanors.

    TRUE   FALSE